THE
SUPERVICTIM
SYNDROME

► THE
► SUPERVICTIM
► SYNDROME

How to
Break
the Cycle

► THOMAS R. McCABE, PH.D.

JOHNSON ◇ INSTITUTE®
Minneapolis

THE SUPERVICTIM SYNDROME
How to Break the Cycle

Cover Design: Lecy Design

Library of Congress Cataloging-in-Publication Data

McCabe, Thomas R.
    The supervictim syndrome : how to break the cycle / by
Thomas R. McCabe.
        p.   cm.
    ISBN 1-56246-008-0
    1. Helplessness (Psychology) 2. Self-defeating behavior.
3. Psychology, Pathological. I. Title.
    RC455.4.S43M33 1991
    616.85 ' 8—dc20   91-184
                                                            CIP

Printed in the United States of America.

To Pat and "T. P."

▶ CONTENTS

▶ INTRODUCTION

This booklet is about victims. It would be difficult to think of a more timely topic, as this seems to be the age of victims. The news is full of events in which people are victimized in one way or another—robberies, muggings, rapes, murders, terrorist attacks and so on— events that are happening with increasing frequency.

This booklet is not about victims in the ordinary sense, however, but about people suffering the effects of a related yet distinct phenomenon I call the *supervictim syndrome*. Victims of the types of incidents mentioned above are usually passive recipients; things happen to them, and usually they recover and get on with their lives. However, the other type of victims, those I term *supervictims,* are usually active participants; things happen to them, too, but they don't recover. As a result of early experiences in which they have been victimized, they learn to think of themselves as victims and unwittingly help to perpetuate this role.

This perpetuation of one's role as a victim is what I refer to as the supervictim syndrome, and it is at the heart of the problems of more and more people who are seen in counseling and therapy settings these days, from teenagers struggling with issues of identity or self-esteem to adults feeling shame rooted in dysfunctional families of origin. Being a victim is largely out of one's control, but you can be victorious in overcoming the supervictim syndrome. This book will help you to determine if you are a supervictim; to identify the feelings and behaviors that are part of the supervictim syndrome, including the ones that keep you stuck in that role; and to overcome that destructive syndrome, emerging as a victor, the master of your soul.

▶ 1
▶ What Is a
▶ Supervictim?

Most, if not all, of the people living today have been or will be victims at some point in their lives, some more often than once. Being victimized is almost part and parcel of living in today's world. Each year thirty-five million Americans are victims of the following types of incidents and situations:

- ▶ Robbery
- ▶ Rape or assault
- ▶ Divorce
- ▶ Automobile accident
- ▶ Serious illness

- Business swindle
- Airplane crash
- Terrorist attack or hostage situation
- Natural disaster, such as earthquake, flood, fire, hurricane, and tornado

Destructive and threatening things happen to most of us at various times all through life. That's simply the way it is. The fact that we have been victimized, no matter how many times in early or later life, does not automatically mean that we will develop the supervictim syndrome.

Some who have been victimized, even numerous times, never develop the supervictim syndrome. Phyllis, for example, is a forty-six-year-old divorced woman who came from a family that did not know how to provide her with love, acceptance, or nurture. As a child she did not feel wanted, and she was seldom shown affection. An accident she experienced as a child left her with a minor facial scar. In her school years she had a hard time learning, and she was raped as a teenager. As an adult she was further victimized. She went through a painful divorce, her car was stolen, and more recently her apartment was vandalized. Although her background is typical of many people who have developed the supervictim syndrome, as you will learn by reading further, there is nothing in her behavior that would indicate the presence of this damaging syndrome.

Why is it that someone like Phyllis, who has been victimized numerous times, has not become a supervictim, while others who have had far fewer victim experiences have? The answer is this: The supervictim syndrome is not simply the result of the accumulation of victim experiences. There is a world of difference between what actually has happened to us and how we have learned to react to our experiences.

Those who develop the supervictim syndrome are in many ways double victims, usually victims of sad and unfortunate events in childhood or adolescence and always victims of their own reactions to these events.

The supervictim syndrome is the learned, conditioned mind-set that many persons develop to cope with incidents in which they are victimized. They develop it unconsciously as children and perpetuate it unknowingly as adults.

The supervictim syndrome was first identified several years ago by researchers at Roosevelt Hospital in New York. They noted a "V" pattern (which I tend to think of as standing for "supervictim") in test profiles of some of their patients to whom they administered the Minnesota Multiphasic Personality Inventory (MMPI). Clinicians at this hospital saw the victimization profile as being the result of learned, unrealistic beliefs and expectations. The subjects whose tests displayed the "V" pattern have been described in the following terms: "They were victimized, even though not accepting responsibility for themselves, they were accomplices in their victimization. They . . . were first and foremost victims of their own expectations." I have administered the MMPI to thousands of people in treatment and have noticed this "V" pattern in many test profiles. In therapy the people whose tests display this pattern tend to feel helpless, depressed, angry, and misunderstood. Sometimes on the surface such a person may appear to be docile, calm, and submissive. Yet underneath the person is like a raging volcano, ready to erupt any time with feelings of both bitterness and stubbornness. In relationships these people have a strong feeling of failure, a sense that they have not received what they deserve. No matter how many times they experience disappointment and abuse, however, they do not readjust their expectations. They continue to feel resentful and blame others, yet they cling to the same set of expectations, hoping for different results the next time.

▶2

▶ Why People Develop
▶ the Supervictim Syndrome

The origins of the supervictim syndrome can usually be found in the powerful influences of early life experiences. Young minds are very impressionable and are strongly influenced by victim experiences. Children or adolescents who have been victimized are particularly vulnerable to developing the supervictim syndrome because they often lack a sense of identity, are unable to identify and express their feelings, and cannot establish the sense of self-worth necessary to engage in healthy relationships later in life.

The following types of experiences can lead a person to develop a supervictim syndrome:

- Lack of love, approval, acceptance, and attention
- Being smothered or overprotected
- Ongoing mental abuse
- Ongoing physical abuse
- Ongoing sexual abuse
- Physical or emotional abandonment
- Being treated inconsistently by parents
- Receiving mixed messages from parents or other grownups
- Constantly being shamed or blamed
- Witnessing one's parents' frequent verbal fighting or violence toward one another
- Having a physical handicap
- Having serious health problems
- Having a learning disability
- Severe economic deprivation
- Being a victim of a serious accident or natural disaster

These are "normal" circumstances for many children. Incapable of understanding what is happening and unable to generate self-esteem, children in such circumstances begin to search for strategies to allow them to feel good about themselves, to "win" the love and approval of others, to gain acceptance, to get attention, and to avoid further rejection. They make early decisions about themselves that may last a lifetime. They develop and project a mental image of what life and relationships are all about and of what they must do in the future to meet their own needs.

These children grow up and enter adult life perpetuating the mind-set of faulty beliefs and unrealistic expectations that they developed as children to deal with the experiences that victimized them. Then they approach and engage in adult relationships with that pre-conceived set of expectations. In relationships they look for experiences that support and reinforce their childhood belief systems.

Whether or not you suspect that you are a supervictim, the following self-test will help you understand the types of incidents that can set the stage for the development of the supervictim syndrome.

To get you started thinking about incidents in your childhood or adolescence in which you were victimized, here are some examples from the lives of some of my recent clients.

"I grew up in a home where love and approval weren't expressed by either of my parents, especially my mother."

"My dad left us when I was three. I felt abandoned, as if it was my fault."

"I never felt I was good enough. I couldn't please anyone."

"My parents were divorced when I was six. I thought I was responsible for it."

"I was emotionally abused. I was always told that I wasn't wanted, mostly by my dad."

"All the years I was growing up I was blamed for everything."

"My sister accused me and my parents believed her because she was their favorite."

"From the time I was in junior high my parents, but especially my dad, always compared me with my brother, particularly in terms of sports ability."

"I am the victim of incest. My stepfather and grandfather both abused me from the time I was nine until I was thirteen or fourteen."

"The kids at school always made fun of me because I was tall for my age and overweight."

"In school several teachers constantly reminded me that I wasn't as bright as my older sister. This was mostly in the third and fifth grades."

"Even in grade school I remember feeling this tremendous fear of rejection."

"I lost partial use of my left arm in a car accident when I was eight. The accident was caused by a drunk driver."

"When I was fifteen I was raped by a man I didn't know."

"My parents and I lost all our possessions in a flood when I was six."

"When I was five we moved, and all my toys were lost, including my favorite doll."

Self-Test:
Are You a Candidate for the Supervictim Syndrome?

➡ As a child, did you experience any of the following?

___ Lack of love, approval, acceptance, and attention
___ Being smothered or overprotected
___ Ongoing mental abuse
___ Ongoing physical abuse
___ Ongoing sexual abuse
___ Physical or emotional abandonment
___ Being treated inconsistently by your parents
___ Receiving mixed messages from your parents or other grownups
___ Constantly being shamed or blamed

___ Witnessing your parents' frequent verbal and/or physical violence toward one another
___ Having a physical handicap
___ Having serious health problems
___ Having a learning disability
___ Severe economic deprivation
___ Being a victim of a serious accident or natural disaster

➡ Describe the incidents you have checked above. Write down the circumstances corresponding to the incident, the people involved, how old you were at the time, whether the incident was an isolated event or ongoing, and your feelings about it.

_____

_____

_____

_____

_____

_____

_____

_____

_____

_____

➡ List below any other experiences you had as a victim when you were a child.

_____

_____

_____

_____

_____

_____

If you can cite a number of examples of the types of incidents listed above, your background may have set the stage for you to develop the supervictim syndrome. In the next section we will see if that has, in fact, been the case for you.

▶ 3

▶ How People Encourage
▶ the Supervictim Syndrome

Usually the supervictim syndrome manifests itself in either of two extremes. Some persons with this syndrome come to believe that they have unlimited power and are able to "fix," take care of, and control others. Feeling so powerful, they assume responsibility for the welfare and behavior of other people. Others with the supervictim syndrome become helpless. They believe they are absolutely powerless; having no power of their own, they do everything they can to please others, looking to other people for self-worth, approval, and validation.

It is this all-or-nothing belief that keeps people in the cycle of the supervictim syndrome, engaged in self-defeating behaviors and trapped with the accompanying feelings of shame, guilt, fear, insecurity, anger, self-pity, and despair. With this all-or-nothing belief, they become totally focused on either manipulating or taking care of others, and this mind-set incapacitates their ability to identify and attend to their own needs.

Unless these persons identify their painful feelings and victimizing beliefs and behaviors and directly and consistently confront and change them, they may spend their lives trapped in the supervictim syndrome.

Barbara, a young housewife, is a typical example. Her parents had serious emotional problems. They had difficulty showing love and affection. They were constantly bickering and putting each other down, and both had extramarital affairs. They were inconsistent with Barbara; one minute they would tell her she was special and beautiful, and the next minute they would tell her she was stupid and ugly. Barbara recalls no physical or sexual abuse, but she vividly remembers the mixed messages from her parents, the constant family conflicts, and the unhappiness she felt growing up.

Somewhere along the way, Barbara developed her mind-set, a belief that, when the time came for her to get married, there were not going to be any conflicts or problems. She was going to make her husband and children happy and make sure the members of her family showed lots of love to one another. Part of her mind-set was the assumption that she had the power to make others happy by her example and efforts.

Today Barbara is very unhappy because the expectations that grew out of her mind-set are not being met. Despite her efforts, she had many problems and major conflicts with her husband and their two children. She is currently in therapy, looking at the origins of her unrealistic mind-set and exploring her feelings of powerlessness. She has the super-victim syndrome.

Characteristics of the Supervictim Syndrome

Because the supervictim syndrome comes in many guises, there are various ways to understand its dynamics. It may be easier to understand if we look at some of its characteristics:

- ▸ Learned helplessness
- ▸ Control
- ▸ Repeatedly finding oneself a victim
- ▸ Having a negative attitude toward one-

self and others
- ‣ Seeing oneself as degraded
- ‣ Having self-defeating behaviors

Learned Helplessness

A look at the results of various animal experiments may help explain learned helplessness. In one such experiment, a research psychologist and his colleagues placed dogs in locked cages. The dogs were given electrical shocks at random intervals. The dogs tried to escape the shocks but could not. They quickly learned that, no matter what they did, they could not control the shocks. When nothing they did stopped the shocks, they stopped trying to escape. They gave up and became passive, compliant, and submissive.

Even when the cage doors were left open and they could escape—even when they were shown the way out—they did not attempt to leave the cages. Researchers call this phenomenon learned helplessness. They claim that the earlier in life the dogs were subjected to such treatment, the longer their resistance lasted.

Similarly, whenever we humans believe that we are helpless over what happens to us, we give up and become passive. This belief reinforces the supervictim syndrome.

John is a twenty-eight-year-old electrical

engineer. He reports that in his early life he experienced "tons of rejections," both at home and with his classmates. He gradually victimized himself with a mind-set that he was never going to have a successful relationship as an adult and that he was always going to be rejected.

He recently began group therapy. "Who would ever want to have a relationship with me?" he first asked the group. He shared his hurt and pain over numerous rejections during the past few years from dating experiences. Now that he's in therapy John is finally beginning to understand his supervictim syndrome. He's beginning to see how he continues to victimize himself with the mind-set he developed a long time ago. He goes into every new relationship with the expectation that he will be rejected and usually does things that bring about the rejection. John's is a self-fulfilling prophecy: He sets himself up for rejection. And each new rejection reinforces his assumption that he is unlovable and unacceptable, perpetuating the cycle. John has the supervictim syndrome.

Control

We can also understand the dynamics of the supervictim syndrome by looking at the characteristic of control. Trying to control the uncontrollable is probably the primary feature of the supervictim syndrome. Sometimes supervictims are aware that they are trying to control or are being controlled by others. Methods of controlling others include physical threats, manipulations, trickery, and emotional blackmail.

At other times it is not so obvious, and supervictims can be genuinely confused as to what they can and cannot control. The control may even be disguised in the form of being obsessed by and worrying about people and things, as both of these mental activities can give us a false sense of security and a feeling of control. For example, Maryanne's husband has a job that requires extensive highway driving, and she worries constantly about his safety. As she recently said, "Sure, I worry. I'm worried to death. But if I don't worry, he may have an accident. It shows that I care about his safety."

Think about it. Does the fact that Maryanne worries have anything to do with the possibility that her husband will have an accident? Of course it doesn't. It just proves that Maryanne knows how to worry, and it gives her a sense of control.

Which of the following can we control: The weather? Our weight? Our age? Our death? Someone else's death? The way we dress? How someone else treats us? What we say to someone? And how about our feelings? Do we control our feelings? If not, who does?

Repeatedly Finding Oneself a Victim

Yet another way to appreciate the way in which the supervictim syndrome develops is to look at supervictims' daily conversational exchanges. They act and react in one of three roles in their transactions with other people—the role of rescuer, victim, or persecutor. They play various roles at different times and may not be aware of which roles they are playing at any given time. They can switch back and forth, even in the same conversation with another person. They may attempt to rescue someone, then slip into the role of victim when the rescue attempt is unappreciated, and subsequently assume the role of persecutor.

Look at a typical transaction between Maria and her husband, Carlos:

> **Maria:** Today I worked on the checking account statement and finally got the thing straightened out.
> **Carlos:** You should have left the job for me!
> **Maria:** No matter how I try to help, you make me feel that I'm not capable.
> **Carlos:** I was only trying to save you some frustration.
> **Maria:** Next time you can do it yourself!

Does this conversation sound familiar? You can see how Maria went from rescuer to victim to persecutor, all in one brief conversation. This sequence is repeated constantly. Maria ends up feeling like a victim, unappreciated and misunderstood. Yet, as emotionally painful as the victim role is, Maria will probably continue in the rescuer-victim-persecutor cycle because it reinforces her early mind-set regarding her life. So she may contemplate new strategies, perhaps determined to try harder next time. But she will not seriously consider making any real changes in the way she interacts with Carlos. Maria too has the supervictim syndrome.

Having a Negative Attitude Toward Oneself and Others

The supervictim syndrome also manifests itself in the negative either/or attitudes that those who are supervictims tend to have about themselves and others. Some supervictims have the attitude "I'm not OK, but you are OK," with the unspoken feeling "I need to get love and approval from you so that I can feel OK."

Tom, for example, is a junior high school student who has been raised in a verbally abusive family. He has no sense of self-worth and presents himself as inadequate, helpless, and "needy." He assumes that other people are somehow emotionally healthier than he is, and he believes that someone or something will come along and save him—and that, in turn, will prove that he is "OK" and worthy of love. Tom certainly has the supervictim syndrome.

Others with the supervictim syndrome have the attitude "I'm not OK, and you aren't OK either." Accompanying this attitude is the unexpressed feeling "You don't know that you're not OK, and rather than focus on my own problems and needs, I'll concentrate on fixing you, and by doing that I'll feel OK about myself."

Even though Harry has never felt good about himself, he continues to focus his energies on his wife. He knows that she has problems, so he is forever trying to make her feel good about herself. On the one hand he admits that it isn't working and that he feels very frustrated; but rather than address possible solutions to his own problems, he is still focusing all his energies on his wife, somehow expecting different results. Harry has the supervictim syndrome.

Seeing Oneself as Degraded

Another element of the supervictim syndrome is focusing upon one's degradation. In describing their experience of this aspect of the syndrome, people will sometimes use the word *doormat*. Susan, a new member of the support group, says, "All my life I've felt like a doormat, always being walked on." She is still unaware of her strong need for approval. She tells about all kinds of self-defeating behaviors and instances in which she has been taken advantage of by others. Yet to this day, she continues behaving like a doormat, drawn to relationships in which she'll most likely be victimized. Obviously Susan has the super-victim syndrome.

Another example is Marilyn, a seventeen-year-old who is currently in treatment. She feels emotionally abused in almost all her relationships and feels she has never received what she deserves in a relationship. No matter how hard she tries to be a perfect daughter, she can never seem to please her parents. She struggles for acceptance at school, too, but feels rejected by her peers. Desperate for affection and acceptance, she became sexually active at the age of fifteen, but though she did everything she could to please her boyfriend, he recently dumped her for someone else. Yet no matter how many times she has been disappointed, she has not readjusted her set of expectations. She clings to the same expectations, hoping for different results the next time. She still has the fantasy that one day her relationship with her parents will become warm and nurturing, that she'll find a "best friend" she can pour out her heart to and a boyfriend who's a perfect soulmate, that some good person will see her despair and come to her rescue. Marilyn too has the supervictim syndrome.

Other Self-Defeating Behaviors

One way to view some of the dynamics of the supervictim syndrome is to look at the characteristics of a self-defeating personality:

- ‣ Choosing people and situations that lead to failure or mistreatment even when better options are clearly visible.
- ‣ Rejecting or rendering ineffective the attempts of others to help.
- ‣ Responding to positive events with guilt or behavior that produces pain.
- ‣ Inciting angry or rejecting responses from others, then feeling hurt and rejected.
- ‣ Rejecting opportunities for pleasure or being reluctant to acknowledge enjoying oneself.
- ‣ Failure to accomplish tasks crucial to personal objectives despite demonstrated ability to do so.
- ‣ Being uninterested in or rejecting people who consistently treat one well.

▶ Engaging in excessive self-sacrifice that is unsolicited by the intended recipient.

Continuous self-defeating behavior is a hallmark of the supervictim syndrome.

Self-Test: Do You Have the Supervictim Syndrome?

To tell if you have the supervictim syndrome, first review your self-test regarding instances in which you were a victim (see the self-test in Chapter 2). This will help you to appreciate the experiences that could have set the stage for your movement into the supervictim syndrome.

Now list the feelings, beliefs, and behaviors operating in your life that may be manifestations of the supervictim syndrome.

Feelings

➡ List the negative feelings that you have the most difficulty dealing with. For example, do you have constant feelings of guilt, shame, depression, anger, inadequacy, worry, low self-esteem, or fear?

_____ _____

_____ _____

_____ _____

_____ _____

➡ Where did all these feelings come from? Do you recognize some of them as your responses to experiences you had in childhood? Write your answer below.

_____

_____

_____

_____

_____

_____

_____

_____

Beliefs
➡ Do you believe any of the following? (Use this list to start, recognizing that you might have similar beliefs that should be listed in the space below.)

____ I am helpless to meet my own needs
____ It is my responsibility to make him or her happy
____ I have to do it perfectly
____ I need his or her love and approval
____ I'm selfish if I think of myself
____ I have no right to speak up
____ I need to prove myself

___ I am the same as my behavior
___ I can't stand conflict or arguing
___ I can't say "no"
___ I'm responsible for his or her feelings
___ I need everyone to like me

➡ Now list some beliefs you have that the above section of this booklet has led you to think may be part of a supervictim syndrome.

_____

_____

_____

_____

_____

_____

_____

_____

Behaviors
➡ Do you exhibit any of the following behaviors? (Again, be aware that this is a partial list.)

___ I don't speak up
___ I allow others to control me
___ I give in all the time
___ I let my fear stop me from acting

___ I allow others' anger to intimidate me
___ I avoid confrontations
___ I berate myself when I make a mistake
___ I compare myself to others
___ I don't take risks where I may be rejected
___ I don't let people get close for fear of rejection
___ I refuse to ask for any kind of help

➡ Now list examples of other behaviors that may be part of a supervictim syndrome.

_____

_____

_____

_____

_____

_____

_____

_____

_____

If your first self-test indicated that you had a number of victim experiences as a child or adolescent and if you checked or listed a number of negative feelings, beliefs, or behaviors in the above self-test, you may well be caught in a supervictim syndrome.

If You Are
a Supervictim

The biggest challenge for those who want to recover from the supervictim syndrome is identifying, sharing, and "owning" their feelings, then changing their unrealistic thinking and expectations and the self-defeating behaviors that are the basis of the supervictim syndrome. If you have realized that you are a supervictim as a result of taking the above self-test or while reading this booklet, the next chapter will help you identify the things you do that keep you stuck in the cycle represented by the supervictim syndrome.

▶4

▶ Why People Get Stuck in
▶ the Supervictim Syndrome

To admit to being a supervictim is difficult, and to stop being one is even more difficult. Once supervictims admit their situation, it's time to make a decision: Do they choose to stay this way, or do they dare to change?

Many people who are caught in the supervictim syndrome stay stuck there for the rest of their lives, struggling in a mind-set that keeps them looking to other people to give meaning and purpose to their lives. Six factors tend to keep people stuck in their supervictim syndrome:

- ▸ Belief that they have no choice
- ▸ Fear of change
- ▸ Reluctance to give up the benefits of staying in the syndrome
- ▸ Ignorance of the games they are playing
- ▸ Continuous negative self-talk
- ▸ Avoidance of responsibility

Belief That They Have No Choice

First of all, to remain stuck people must continue to believe that there is no choice. If they were to entertain options, their belief system would begin to crumble. They must firmly hold on to their all-or-nothing belief, either a belief in their extreme powerfulness or a belief in their extreme helplessness, in order for their supervictim role to continue to seem a normal way of life. They must firmly hold on to the belief that their needs are best met by being emotionally focused and dependent on others.

Once people with the supervictim syndrome admit there are options, it forces them to make a decision: Do I choose to remain in the supervictim syndrome, or dare to risk change? The mere suggestion that they are choosing to be victims usually makes these people bristle. They strongly deny that this is so, resisting the possibility. Before they became aware that they might be choosing to be victims they were passively participating in their own victimization; now they are actively participating.

James was furious when a friend told him that he didn't have to put up with the obnoxious and defiant behavior of his son. He offered reasons why he had to tolerate it. James is choosing to remain stuck in the supervictim syndrome.

Shawna's husband embarrassed her, yelling and using obscene language in public—and it wasn't the first time it had happened. Yet she became defensive and even protective of her husband when a girlfriend mentioned that she didn't have to tolerate that behavior. "You don't understand. I have no choice," she angrily retorted. Yet ironically Shawna had made a choice; she had chosen to remain stuck in the supervictim syndrome.

Fear of Change

The second factor is the fear of change. Most people don't particularly like to change. In fact, it seems a paradox in life that, while people verbalize the desire for change, they unconsciously wish to preserve the status quo. A fear of the unknown keeps people the way they are. It provides a false sense of security, a sense that they are in control of things.

Dorothy, for example, admits that she is in a relationship with her boyfriend that is going nowhere. Yet she continues it for "security," fearful of ending it and feeling abandoned again. "After all," she once rationalized, "the devil you know is better than the one you don't know."

Reluctance to Give Up the Benefits

It is the third factor that perhaps keeps most people in the supervictim syndrome, the reluctance to give up the benefits of victimization. And let there be no doubt about it: There are benefits. The question that such a person needs to ask is, "What am I getting out of continuing this?"

It is important to acquire and admit an awareness of the benefits received by choosing to be a victim. The benefits can include the following:

Attention. Granted, it's usually negative and painful attention, but it may be perceived as preferable to no attention at all. Many people feel it's better to be hurt than ignored.

Looking back now, Frieda can remember when she was "active" in her supervictim syndrome, thinking that her husband didn't love her anymore after he stopped physically abusing her.

Identity. The supervictim syndrome gives a person an identity, and it can be a defense against having no self-identity. Some people have no identity except their victim identity, that of "slave," "scapegoat," "doormat," or "gofer."

For example Frank, a sixteen year old, is the family scapegoat. He always gets blamed for the mischievous behavior of his brothers and sisters. He says, "Everybody's always picking on me. I can't seem to do anything right." The only identity he feels that he has, as he put it to his therapy group, is as "a screw-up."

Security. Remaining in the supervictim syndrome is safe and predictable. The world makes sense; frustration and rejection are just around the corner. In a way it's comfortable knowing how things are going to end up.

Martha, who has been involved in several relationships in which she has been abused, says, "I'm used to it. I've been through it so many times before." How she relates to her boyfriends and the results of the relationships are totally predictable, and there's some comfort in that very predictability.

Ignorance of the Games They Are Playing

A fourth factor in remaining in the supervictim syndrome is people's ignorance of the games they are playing. Most people have some understanding of the concept of "games." They may put different labels on them, but the concept is not new, as evidenced by the frequent comment by many people, "I don't want to play games with you!"

People who are supervictims need to look at the deadly games they continuously end up playing in their interpersonal relationships—games that are cyclic, repeated time after time, keeping them stuck in the supervictim syndrome.

Some of the common games supervictims play are these:

- ▶ Ain't It Awful
- ▶ Poor Me
- ▶ I Was Only Trying to Help
- ▶ See How Hard I Tried
- ▶ No One Appreciates Me
- ▶ Kick Me

Jane recently admitted to the group that she had been playing Kick Me with her husband. She sets up the game so that he will "kick" her and she will end up feeling rejected. She does not express her feelings of irritation and annoyance about his inconsiderate and rude behavior. Instead of expressing these feelings directly to him, she says and does little things that she knows will enrage him.

When he retaliates with rage, she has learned to get personal satisfaction from feeling terribly mistreated by him, as if she had been kicked.

Continuous Negative Self-Talk

A fifth factor, negative self-talk, is extremely important. Self-talk is the constant internal dialogue that human beings engage in. Self-talk, either positive or negative, is the critical shaper of our feelings. Years and years of negative self-talk can cripple people, keeping them in and strongly reinforcing the super-victim syndrome as a mind-set for life. Negative self-talk includes the following internal statements:

- ▸ That's the way I am
- ▸ I'm stupid (ugly, bad)
- ▸ I'm a terrible husband/wife
- ▸ I'm an awful mother/father
- ▸ I'm a lousy son/daughter
- ▸ It's too late to change
- ▸ It's too hard to change
- ▸ I can't change
- ▸ It's no use

Avoidance of Responsibility

The sixth factor is avoidance of responsibility. People can get a lot of mileage out of feeling sorry for themselves or feeling "put-upon." They can whine, complain, find fault, be long-suffering, and wallow in self-pity. The bottom line is that their energy is consumed in being upset about what is being done to them rather than in taking responsibility to change.

George, for example, is in declining health due to his workaholism. He works fourteen hours a day to provide things he thinks his wife wants. He talks constantly about the sacrifices he makes for his wife, forever complaining, "She doesn't appreciate a thing I do." He is avoiding the responsibility of taking care of his health and maintaining a satisfying relationship with his wife.

Self-Test:
What's Keeping You Stuck in the Supervictim Syndrome?

Focusing upon each of the above factors, check off or list the things that are keeping you stuck as a volunteer in the supervictim syndrome.

Choice
➡ Can you admit that you are choosing to be a supervictim and that you play an active role in what is happening in your life?
Yes ____   No ____

➡ Do you believe that you can control what you think and feel and how you act?

Yes _____ No _____

➡ Do you believe that you can control what others think and feel and how they act?

Yes _____ No _____

Fears

➡ What specific fears of change keep you stuck in the supervictim syndrome? Try completing the following statement: "If I change the way I do this or that, . . ." What do you assume will happen?

_____

_____

_____

_____

_____

_____

_____

Benefits

➡ What are your payoffs for remaining in the supervictim syndrome? Examples are: "It's the only way I can get his/her attention" or "I can feel sorry for myself."

_____

_____

_____

_____

_____

_____

_____

_____

Games

➡ List the games you catch yourself playing.
Make up your own labels and initials for these
games. Some examples are below.

IBDOA	I've Been Dumped on Again
IKEITBD	I Keep Expecting It to Be Different
IDEFU	I Do Everything for You
BTSIMFU	Boy, the Sacrifices I've Made for You

_____

_____

_____

_____

_____

_____

_____

Negative Self-Talk

➡ Listen to your inner dialogue and record any language about yourself or others that is negative or accusatory. Examples are below.

I'm a failure
She shouldn't have
It isn't fair
I'm a terrible person
He has no right

_____

_____

_____

_____

_____

_____

_____

Avoidance of Responsibility

➡ List the ways you avoid responsibility for change. These are usually things you do that consume the energy you could be using to change. For example, "I get so wrapped up in other people's troubles that I can avoid dealing with my own."

_____

_____

_____

_____

_____

_____

_____

_____

_____

➡ After seeing the consequences of choosing to be a supervictim, do you want to stay stuck in this syndrome?

Yes _____   No _____

▶ 5

▶ How To Break the Cycle

While the awareness of options is the first step in the process of change, this awareness is not enough. Carla, for example, admits that she still chooses to be stuck. "You know me," she said. "I guess I ask for it. I've always taken responsibility for everyone's problems and for everyone's feelings." Yet she is making no effort to change. She recognizes her status but doesn't appear to accept it. Recognition and acceptance are not simultaneous events for many people.

But once people both admit and accept that they are doing this to themselves, they immediately begin the process of empowering themselves. They can see themselves preparing for a voyage to victory once they get rid of the mind-set that "somebody is doing something to me" and shake off that "poor me" mentality. The voyage to victory begins, however, not the moment they admit and accept that they are choosing to be supervictims, but the moment they commit to the process of changing by developing a specific plan of change.

Developing a Plan

The successful plan includes elements to change the supervictims' feelings, ways of thinking, and behavior patterns, for changes in all of these are necessary in order to get out of the supervictim syndrome. Now is a good time to start developing the components of such a plan.

Feelings

In developing your plan, be aware of your incapacitating and immobilizing feelings—feelings such as shame, anger, guilt, fear, and worry. It's important that you make yourself share them with another person and also that you make sure you own them. A very common problem supervictims have is that they share feelings, but rather than owning them, they project them. For instance, they often project their feelings of anger by saying to a friend or loved one, "You made me upset when you . . ." Instead you should own responsibility for your anger and other negative feelings by saying, "I got myself upset when you . . ." We create our feelings and are responsible for them. Once we own our feelings, we can change them.

Examples of incapacitating feelings and how we might plan to deal with them are as follows.

Feeling: Fear of change.
How to deal with it: I will allow myself to feel the fear of change, but I will walk through the fear, remembering that fear confronted is fear quickly diminished.

Feeling: Worry.
How to deal with it: I realize that worry has given me a false sense of control. Rather than worrying and blaming others for "making" me worry I will realize that I create my own feelings of worry and will begin to separate the "possibilities" from the "probabilities" of future events and will be concerned rather than worried about the probabilities only, not about the mere possibilities.

Now list your incapacitating feelings, how you project many of them, and how you plan to own them and deal with them:

➡ *Feeling:* _____
➡ *How to deal with it:*

_____

_____

_____

_____

_____

_____

_____

_____

_____

_____

➡ *Feeling:* _____
➡ *How to deal with it:*

_____

_____

_____

_____

_____

_____

_____

_____

_____

_____

➥ *Feeling:* _____
➥ *How to deal with it:*

_____

_____

_____

_____

_____

_____

_____

_____

_____

Beliefs

It is also important that you be aware of the victimizing beliefs you have learned that produce the sorts of feelings described above. The plan is to reprogram yourself, eradicating self-defeating beliefs, expectations, and self-talk and replacing them with victorious ones. For example, it is important to get rid of the belief "I need his or her love/approval/attention" and replace it with the more realistic thought "I wish I had his or her love/approval/attention, but I sure don't have to have it." You must stop demanding approval and attention. A more victorious belief is "It is more important for me to love, affirm, accept, and nurture myself than to be loved, affirmed, accepted, and nurtured by anyone else."

You need to replace your all-or-nothing mind-set with clear ideas of what and where your power is and isn't. You must change the negative things you have the power to change and accept the things over which you are powerless.

It is important that you watch your expectations. Do you expect other people to make you happy? Do you assume that you have the power to make other people happy?

It is also important that you replace your negative self-talk with positive self-talk that validates you, such as "I am lovable and capable." You must keep reminding yourself that you were not born with a supervictim syndrome; it is not innate or in your blood. You learned it, and what you learned you can unlearn, though it will take work.

An example of a supervictim belief and how you might plan to deal with it is as follows.

Belief: I can't stand to be abandoned.

How to deal with it: A relationship doesn't have to work out. If I am abandoned I can stand it; it will be sad, but it won't be the end of the world. I choose not to be in a relationship that is not good for me or one in which I am not wanted. I don't have to be in a relationship to feel worthwhile or good about myself.

Now list your supervictim beliefs and how you plan to deal with them.

➡ *Belief:* _____

➡ *How to deal with it:*

_____

_____

_____

_____

_____

_____

_____

_____

_____

➡ *Belief:* _____

➡ *How to deal with it:*

_____

_____

_____

_____

_____

_____

_____

_____

➡ Belief: _____

➡ How to deal with it:

_____

_____

_____

_____

_____

_____

_____

_____

Behavior

The plan is to eliminate both passive and aggressive behaviors, replacing them with assertive behaviors. It is important for you to remember that you have the right to stand up for yourself, to express your wants, wishes, and desires. You may not get all the things you want, but other people will at least be aware of your wishes. If you have trouble speaking up, you can enroll in assertiveness training courses. Remember that you are responsible for your own behavior, not the behavior of the other person.

An example of a supervictim behavior and how you might plan to deal with it is as follows.

Behavior: Difficulty saying "no."

How to deal with it: I can say "no" just as easily as I can say "yes." They are both one-syllable words. I will set limits as to what I am and am not willing to do and let them be known. I can rehearse saying "no" so that it will be easier to do when it is in my best interest. I can think of how saying "no" will make my life better. The other person may not like it when I say "no," but that is really his or her problem and not mine.

Now list your supervictim behaviors and how you plan to deal with them.

➥ *Behavior:* _____

➥ *How to deal with it:*

_____

_____

_____

_____

_____

_____

_____

_____

_____

_____

➡ *Behavior:* _____
➡ *How to deal with it:*

_____

_____

_____

_____

_____

_____

_____

_____

➡ *Behavior:* _____
➡ *How to deal with it:*

_____

_____

_____

_____

_____

_____

_____

_____

Developing Strategies
to Make Your Plan Work

After you have written out your plan, but before you implement it, take time to remember the ways you have sabotaged such efforts in the past. That should help you to avoid sabotaging this plan. Also keep in mind the following four suggestions.

1. Don't expect a "quick fix." Developing a victorious mind-set takes time and practice, practice, and more practice.

2. Don't expect perfection of yourself. Be prepared to experience occasional setbacks or relapses. What you can reasonably expect of yourself is gradual improvement. Be sure to congratulate yourself for the slightest improvement and celebrate it.

3. Don't try to do it alone. Participate in an appropriate self-help program, such as a twelve-step group, or seek individual therapy. You alone can do it, but you can't do it alone.

4. Be aware of your motives for changing. You are not doing it to be noticed, to manipulate others, or to be appreciated by others. In fact, your changes may meet resistance from others, especially initially. You are doing this for yourself.

▶ CONCLUSION

This book has laid the groundwork for change—change that means you *can* break the supervictim cycle. It's now up to you to reclaim your legacy as a person, to "take charge of your vessel" and begin the voyage from supervictim to victor.

Change will not happen overnight. It may take months or even years before you feel you've safely arrived and put your supervictim mind-set behind you. But by starting today, you'll quickly find renewed hope and self-esteem in the journey itself.

Remember, whatever your past, you can control the present and set your future course. Once you decide to leave victimization behind, a whole new life will open up to you. You will discover, perhaps for the first time, that you are worth the effort.

Start today, and proclaim over and over the words of the poet W.C. Henley:

I am the master of my fate,
I am the captain of my soul.

▶ FOR FURTHER READING

Alberti, Robert and Michael Emmons. *Your Perfect Right: A Guide to Assertive Living.* San Luis Obispo, Calif.: Impact, 1990.

Cavanaugh, Eunice. *Understanding Shame: Why It Hurts, How It Helps, How You Can Use It to Transform Your Life.* Minneapolis: Johnson Institute, 1989.

Hayes, Jody. *Smart Love: A Co-Dependency Recovery Program.* Los Angeles: Jeremy P. Tarcher, 1989.

Kaufman, Gershen and Lev Raphael. *Stick Up for Yourself: Every Kid's Guide to Personal Power and Positive Self-Esteem.* Minneapolis: Free Spirit, 1990.

Larson, Earnest. *How to Understand and Overcome Depression.* Liguori, Mo.: Liguori Publications, 1977.

Palmer, Pat with Melissa Alberti Froehner. *Teen Esteem: A Self-Direction Manual for Young Adults.* San Luis Obispo, Calif.: Impact, 1989.

For Order Information,
Call **Toll-Free**

In Minnesota: 1-800-247-0484
In United States: 1-800-231-5165
In Canada: 1-800-447-6660
